BECOMING
A
DISCIPLE
MAKER

THE PURSUIT OF LEVEL 5
DISCIPLE MAKING

BOBBY HARRINGTON
& GREG WIENS

DEDICATION

This book is dedicated to the disciple makers who worked with us to develop the Disciple Maker Assessment framework:

- Jim Putman – and Real Life Ministries
- Bill Hull – and the Bonhoeffer Project
- Todd Wilson – and the Exponential team
- Ralph Moore – and the Hope Chapel Movement
- Robby Gallaty – and the Replicate Ministries team
- Monte Stark – and the Life–on–Life Missional Discipleship Team
- Dave Buehring – and the LionShare team
- Luke Yetter – and the Relational Discipleship Network
- Michelle Eagle, Geary Tanner, Josh Patrick – and the Discipleship.org team

CONTENTS

RENEW

RENEWING THE TEACHINGS OF JESUS
TO FUEL DISCIPLE MAKING

CONTINUING THE CONVERSATION...

This book was original written as a part of a series of books for Exponential, a church-planting network. For your reference, Exponential champions the three dimensions of multiplication:

1. Disciple making
2. Capacity building for disciple making
3. Mobilization for disciple making

When these three dimensions align, we get biblical disciples that make biblical disciples who plant churches that plant churches. We get followers who are fully surrendered, putting Jesus at the center of their lives. When we pursue these three areas, we mobilize a movement of missionaries to carry the fullness of Jesus into every nook and cranny of society.

Exponential, in partnership with ministries like Discipleship. org and Healthy Growing Churches, is developing certified online assessment tools to measure an individual's strengths in each of the three dimensions of multiplication, as well as a church's strengths. Discipleship.org is excited to be Exponential's chosen partner for these disciple-making tools.

This eBook centers on the first and most critical dimension in the 3D multiplication model and provides a description of the framework used in this new tool, the Disciple Makers Online Assessment.

Disciple Making That Leads to Multiplication

That is our big prayer here—to see a disciple-making movement resulting in new communities of faith. We believe that the *movemental* dynamic of disciples who make disciples who plant churches that plant churches is part of the multiplication vision that Jesus gave His disciples in Matthew 28:19-20 and in Acts 1:8.

But you will receive power when the Holy Spirit comes on you; and you will be my witnesses in Jerusalem, and in all Judea and Samaria, and to the ends of the earth.

Jesus gave his disciples (both past and present) the power of his Holy Spirit for the ultimate purpose of disciple making that leads to multiplication.

You're now part of this ongoing multiplication conversation. We're thankful you're here, learning about disciple making. It is truly the Master's call to anyone who says they want to follow him.

We hope you'll soon discover and agree with us that this book, *Becoming a Disciple Maker*, is a critical resource in fueling the church multiplication conversation.

INTRODUCTION

In late 2016, a group of national disciple-making experts gathered to spend time developing a paradigm by which people could evaluate their effectiveness as disciple makers. We received input from seasoned leaders, female and male alike, and were especially pleased to have venerable voices like Robert Coleman (author of *The Master Plan of Evangelism*) and others. Those nationally known disciple makers who rolled up their sleeves to help set the framework of this disciple-making tool included:

- Bill Hull, author and founder of The Bonhoeffer Project.
- Jim Putman, author, pastor and co-founder of the Relational Discipleship Network
- Robby Gallaty, author, pastor and founder of Replicate Ministries
- Ralph Moore, author, pastor and founder of the Hope Chapel Movement
- Monte Stark, author, pastor and director of Life on Life Ministries
- Dave Buehring, author, pastor, and founder of LionShare Ministry
- Todd Wilson, author and executive director of Exponential

Other facilitators were involved as well. I (Bobby) led the effort with Todd Wilson's help. My co-author on this book, Greg Wiens, also helped with direction, and then we followed up with the material afterward.

With the help of these and other leaders, we have developed an objective and validated online Disciple Maker Assessment tool.

We have also written this book to explain the tool and the way it gauges disciple makers. Our goal is to help individuals get an accurate perception of themselves as disciple makers so that they can then develop growth plans. We hope to encourage and inspire *everyone* to become Level 5 disciple makers—anyone who makes disciples who then become disciple makers themselves. It's a cycle. We follow Jesus and learn to do what he did.

We have both benefitted greatly from working on this tool and writing about the principles and practices that undergird and support it. Before we go any farther, let us introduce ourselves. We want you to know a little bit about us, which may help you to understand the vantage point we're both writing from and doing life.

I (Bobby) am a lead pastor and church planter. My vantage point has been informed by the following:

- Lead pastor (30 years)
- Church planter
- Coach and trainer of hundreds of church planters
- Founder and director of a national coaching organization for church leaders
- Leader in two national church network systems (Stadia and the Relational Discipleship Network)
- Doctor of Ministry degree in consulting
- Author of numerous books on disciple making, including the popular *DiscipleShift: Five Steps That Help Your Church Make Disciples That Make Disciples* (with Jim Putman and Robert Coleman) and the recently released, *Disciple Maker's Handbook* (with Josh Patrick)
- Co-founder and executive director of Discipleship.org

It was just over ten years ago that I came to the firm conclusion that Jesus' style of disciple making is the core mission of the Church.[1] That awakening now informs everything I do and led me to establish Discipleship.org.

I (Greg) have been a lead pastor, church planter, assessor, and coach. My vantage point has been formed by over thirty-five years of experience, including.

- Lead pastor
- Church planter
- Church, school, and business consultant
- Developer of twenty-plus different assessment tools
- Assistant professor of education (University of Central Florida/Warner Southern University)
- Founder and chief catalyst for Healthy Growing Churches
- Founder and chief catalyst for Healthy Growing Leaders
- Doctorate of Education in psychometrics (University of Central Florida)

I have been an advocate for relational disciple making for the better part of the last four decades. However, at times in my life, I focused more on making disciples rather than intentionally focusing on making disciples who make disciples. I firmly believe there's nothing more important today than being a disciple maker who makes disciples who make disciples—to the fourth generation.

Some Helpful Definitions:

Discipleship.org has adopted a few definitions that many have found useful. They create clarity and give people handles for the disciple making and multiplication conversation. In this book, we're using the following four simple definitions;, they are described in more detail in the book *The Disciple Maker's Handbook.*[2]

- *A disciple* - someone who is following Jesus, being changed by Jesus, and is committed to the mission of Jesus (Matt. 4:19).
- *Disciple making* – entering into relationships to help people to trust and follow Jesus.

- *Disciple maker* - a Christian who enters into relationships with people to help them trust and follow Jesus.
- *Discipleship-first (person/tribe)* - those who see themselves through the missional lens of being disciples who make disciples.

Our Goal

Both Greg and I (Bobby) believe that establishing common markers of the varied approaches to discipleship will be beneficial for the community of disciple-making disciples. We want to avoid elevating one author, method or approach to disciple making over another and instead, create synergy among disciple makers through creating a common language around an online tool.

We also want an online tool to help Christians develop an objective assessment of themselves as disciple makers. By establishing profiles and criteria, we create a benchmark—an objective standard to which we can compare ourselves to the standard of effective disciple makers today.

The practical levels we use are simple and easy to understand and apply—aligning with Exponential's Becoming 5 framework based on five levels of multiplication capacity for churches.[3] Our levels for measuring personal discipleship include:

- Level 1 (Subtracting from disciple-making efforts)
- Level 2 (Plateaued, neither helping nor hindering disciple making)
- Level 3 (Adding, supporting disciple making)
- Level 4 (Reproducing, personally making disciples)
- Level 5 (Multiplying, personally making disciple makers)

Each of these disciple maker levels is unique. We have found that each one has common ways of thinking about God, people, being a disciple, the Kingdom, and what it means to make disciples of Jesus. The more likely someone lives out the Kingdom mindset, practices intentionality, and views their effectiveness from a long-term perspective, the farther they move along the disciple-making scale.

Jesus is our model. Jesus is the pattern for Level 5 disciple makers. He did not just make disciples; he made disciple makers. We both believe that becoming a disciple maker is a really big deal. We have written this book to help you understand our online assessment tool, use it as a map so that you can plot your progress, and pursue further development as a disciple maker. Our passionate prayer is that you'll aspire to become someone who makes disciples who make disciples. We pray you become a Level 5 disciple maker.

Chapter 1

WHY SHOULD I WANT TO BECOME A LEVEL 5 DISCIPLE MAKER?

A disciple maker is a Christian who enters into relationships with people to help them trust and follow Jesus.

The concept of disciple making seems to come into vogue every few decades or so. And then, unfortunately, the pendulum often swings between an intentional effort to help people become new believers (evangelism) and an emphasis on growing disciples (sanctification). It is as if we had to choose between evangelism and spiritual growth. As Jesus showed us in his life and teaching, reaching lost people (evangelism) and helping disciples to grow are both part of discipleship (and disciple making). Evangelism is the front end of disciple making, and spiritual growth is the back end of disciple making. Both are eternally and inextricably linked.[1]

So, making disciples must include relating to people far from Christ in a way that helps them come to faith in Jesus and grow in that faith. Naturally, as they mature, and as they are trained to be intentional disciple makers, they will then repeat the process with others. Discipleship without a healthy element of reaching lost people is not discipleship; it is training for stunted growth Christianity. And what is often thought of as evangelism isn't really evangelism without discipleship; it is head hunting, getting people to make a transaction with God. Essentially, it's simply trying to sell an insurance policy rather than trying to help individuals cross the threshold of faith into a redemptive and growing relationship with God in Christ.

Again, without having and acting on a burden for those who are far from Jesus, growing in that redemptive relationship through Christ is impossible. A century ago, people called it a "soul burden"—a burden for the souls of men and women who are separated from Christ and are experiencing life lived on the edges. It's impossible to truly be transformed through dynamic faith in Christ without wanting to do life with the God of all creation. When you experience the transformation of your life by his love and grace, you're changed eternally.

Jesus Was Intentional

Almost 55 years ago, Robert Coleman wrote the book, *The Master Plan of Evangelism*. It is the gold standard on Jesus' method of disciple making. It sold multiple millions of copies and has been translated into more than 100 languages. Many people do not grasp the nuance of the title: it is not *the Masters' plan*, but *the Master Plan*. Jesus had a master plan; Jesus was intentional, with strategy and an end-result vision.

Intentionality is at the heart of following Jesus' method of disciple making today. This can be hard for some people to embrace. But we have found that disciple makers rely on intentionality. Jesus practiced it, Paul modeled it (2 Timothy 2:2), and the practitioners today swear by it. Intentionality is being deliberate or purposive. It is having and following a plan; it is knowing where to take people and how to help them get there.

Disciple making is love expressed on a journey. Jesus' style of love is not just organic; it is also strategic. In the material below, as you think about Jesus as a disciple maker, make mental notes on his intentionality. Yes, Jesus was organic. But Jesus was intentional. Disciple making is both with intentionality being primary. Jesus was "organically intentional." He was so brilliant at both loving people in their convoluted life situations and in disciple making, that he embodied love and intentionality simultaneously, beautifully and imperceptibly.

Jesus Was a Disciple Maker

As we read the gospels, we see Jesus as the master disciple maker. He spent most of his time and the best of his time in public ministry focused on that one thing. Jesus was all about relating to individuals as people of value. He accepted them where they were, but he didn't leave them there. He loved them in spite of their foibles and, through grace, guided their transformation into a God-centered life.

Peter is a prime example of this. In Matthew's gospel, one moment we see Jesus praise Peter for identifying him as the Messiah, and then in the next moment he accuses Peter of being an ally of the enemy (Matt. 16:16-23). In John 18, Jesus asks Peter, James, and John to pray for and with him during one of his most difficult hours. Then a few minutes later, Jesus chastises Peter for cutting off the ear of the Roman soldier, Malchus. In the same chapter, Peter emphatically states that he would "never" leave Jesus, only to deny ever knowing him that same night. But Jesus never gave up on him. The same man who denied his master three times in a few hours became a founding disciple maker in the Jerusalem Church.

History tells us that Thomas reproduced himself as he traveled many places and eventually gave his life for the cause, in spite of being a doubting personality and one who was hard to convince (John 20:27). It was Phillip who brought Jesus to frustration when he simply couldn't figure out what Jesus was saying (John 14:9). And in John 3, Nicodemus seems to be slow in comprehending the theological concept of being born anew spiritually. Martha was consumed in the details and lost sight of the important things in life (Luke 10:38). Zacchaeus had many shady dealings in his past, but Jesus saw his potential as an influencer of others.

Each of these men and women had their problems, and yet Jesus met them where they were and matured them into disciples, ultimately equipping them to make disciples of others. A person was never a dead end cul-de-sac of ministry for Jesus. He clearly saw their potential for personal transformation, as well as for transforming others after he was gone.

Yet Jesus didn't love these individuals just to see their lives changed. He had a much larger mission in mind. He desired to do what he came to earth to do—to transform their lives for eternity, empowering and equipping them to do the same for others. In the relatively short time that Jesus walked on earth with these faulty faithful few, he intentionally invested in each one to help them nurture an ongoing relationship with the living God—and a relationship that had a profoundly positive impact on everyone who encountered these followers. If we follow what happened to each one, we see that these men and women went on to be used by God to change lives for eternity.

Jesus made disciples who made disciples. Let that sink in. Our Lord didn't just make disciples; *he made disciple makers.* He modeled what he calls us to do. Part of aspiring to be like him is to follow in his example, making disciples who become disciple makers.

Jesus was clear: unless you're intentionally making disciples, you have not yet become a mature disciple. It would have been absurd for Jesus' disciples to think they were *not* responsible for making disciples who made disciples. They didn't need to put it on their to-do checklist. No one had to hold them accountable; making disciples was as natural as breathing. Having heard and seen their Master, they knew they must be intentionally investing their lives in those who would also make disciples. It's what being a disciple is all about. The intentionality piece is big!

In the Book of Acts and the following epistles, we clearly see these same leaders practicing discipleship wherever they went. As they explained who Jesus the Christ was, and as people responded through faith, the early disciples helped these new converts grow in their relationship. In turn, they helped them reproduce their faith and life in others.

The Apostle Paul modeled this behavior so clearly in the sixteen or more churches he planted. He found individuals who would walk beside him—whether they were making tents, starting small groups of followers, or sitting in jail—and helped them reproduce their walk with others. Throughout the New Testament, Paul's name is listed with at least forty-seven men and women that benefitted from Paul's investment in their lives. For Paul, disciple making wasn't a classroom or small group experience; it was a *life* experience! Discipling another was life-on-life wherever he was.

He gives us a glimpse of this disciple making in 1 Thessalonians 2:8: *"…so we cared for you. Because we loved you so much, we were delighted to share with you not only the gospel of God, but our lives as well."* Here, we see how Paul's passion for making disciples of those followers in Thessalonica went much further than simply sharing the Good News of Christ. Additionally, Paul literally lived his transformed life with them so that they could catch how disciples live fully committed to Christ as their Lord. Sharing his life, Paul lived, worked and simply enjoyed people. In the context of doing life with others, he intentionally sought to convey the principles of walking with Christ by faith and then how to transfer what he had learned to others.

No less than seven times in the New Testament, Paul tells those he was discipling to do the same things they saw him do with them while he was with them. Wow! Now that's transparency and authenticity! In 1 Corinthians 11:1, his directive is simple and clear: *"Follow my example, as I follow the example of Christ."*

Writing to the church of Thessalonica, Paul clearly illustrates the whole process of being a disciple who makes disciples that make disciples. In 1 Thessalonians 1:6-7, we find Paul writing to the small church he started, nurtured and then left, saying, *"You became imitators of us and of the Lord, for you welcomed the message in the midst of severe suffering with the joy given by the Holy Spirit. And so you became a model to all the believers in Macedonia and Achaia."* Paul suggests that these followers clearly saw in him a disciple who lived among them, and they welcomed the message, marked by their response of becoming disciples themselves. But the process didn't end there; these followers went on to become models to those who lived around them.

What a wonderful model! Like Jesus before him, Paul not only lived as a disciple with others, he also taught this transference principle to those he discipled. The understanding was clear that they, too, would make disciples. As Paul writes to another one of his disciples, Timothy, he reminds him to keep this reproduction going: *"And the things you have heard me say in the presence of many witnesses entrust to reliable people who will also be qualified to teach others"* (2 Timothy 2:2).

Paul reminds Timothy that not only should he make disciples, but that he should also make disciples who can make disciples who can then make other disciples. Paul sought to live the life that Christ modeled and taught. He exemplified this model and infused this multiplication DNA into every follower. It wasn't about what one person could do, but rather the multiple generations that could result and the cumulative impact they all would have. Throughout the Bible as well as the history of Christianity, people who make disciples don't just look at the short-term impact they can have in people's lives. They're able to see the Kingdom expanded through the long-term impact of making disciples who make disciples. As we will see shortly, this is how eternity-shifting movements have been built.

Jesus, his disciples, and their followers all practiced living the life of a disciple—a life that naturally included making disciples who make disciples. This primary practice that Jesus taught and emulated has never changed.

We Can't Be Like Jesus If We're Not Making Disciples

At the beginning of my junior year of college, a guy from the apartment across the hall shared with me (Greg) what a new life in Christ would look life if I were willing to trust God with my life. As I confessed my sin and began a new life in faith, the Christian campus group I was part of very naturally expected me to be part of a small group of three to four guys who were also new and growing in their faith. I immediately became a part of this group that was healthy, fun and life-giving.

Another expectation of this campus group was that I would share my new faith with those closest to me. I didn't understand it at the time, but the motivation was twofold: those closest to me would see a difference in my life; and others would know of the transforming power of Christ and be open to hearing about it. During the next few weeks, three individuals I shared my experience with crossed that line of faith. Just as Jesus expected his followers to share their faith, this campus organization expected the same thing from me—to help others grow into their faith as I grew spiritually and personally.

So I was barely three weeks old in my walk with Christ, and now I was responsible for these new babes in Christ, which meant that I led a similar small group or Bible study with these three guys. I was only three weeks ahead of my disciples in their growth, but it didn't really matter. It also didn't matter that a couple of these guys were much smarter than me. I was there to coach them in their growth. So for the next eighteen months, I was in my group and also leading a group. Both were simply expectations—a normal part of the disciple-making continuum.

Just as people heard and saw Jesus teach and model disciple making, they also knew they needed to intentionally invest their lives in those who would do the same with others. This is simply what the early church understood a disciple to be. In most churches today, that approach wouldn't pass theological or practical standards. Think whatever you want to, but when I graduated in 1976 with an engineering degree from the University of Michigan, my on-campus experience birthed in me an expectation that post-college I would be involved in a church where I could continue being a disciple and making disciples.

Somehow, in the West, we have adopted a model of ministry that precludes making disciples. I experienced this personally when I left engineering to become a pastor so that I could have more time to make disciples. I went to seminary and found that I wasn't expected to make disciples. Instead, I was expected to be there for the sick and their families, preach sermons, counsel troubled marriages, manage the budget, sit on endless committees, run programs, and make copies of Sunday's bulletin. As the lead pastor, I tried to work with several churches to change this perspective. But to no avail, I failed. I just couldn't change the congregation's expectations of the pastor's role. Eventually, I started my own church but continued to struggle with the pastoral expectations that most churches have.

This irony of this is that Ephesians 4 is very clear about the role of leaders and pastors—to equip (disciple) others to do the things needed in ministry. The role of apostles, prophets, evangelists, shepherds and teachers (APEST) is to make heroes of others, not be your own hero. My gifts were more centered in the apostle range, so I didn't fit the expectation of a shepherd or teacher common to pastors in the previous generation. As I read this passage in Paul's letter to the church in Ephesus, it's clear that God gave us these gifts to equip the body and make it mature, healthy, vibrant and multiplying.

Most church staff are not modeling disciple making. Ironically, that's not expected anywhere else in the church either. By eliminating both the call to and practice of making disciples, we have essentially neutered the Church in the West. Visit any continent in the world other than Europe, North America and Australia, and Christianity is flourishing. In these churches, leaders and followers are not only expected to make disciples, they naturally do it an intentional rhythm of their existence. Christianity is the fastest-growing religion in the world because in all of the other places in the world, the Church is freed up from ministry models devoid of disciple making.

The Core of Every World-Impacting Movement

Within the last twenty centuries, disciple making like Jesus and Paul modeled has ignited and fueled many movements of Christendom—disciples becoming like Christ making disciples of the people they did life with each day. Movements aren't made of professional men and women fulfilling their role in the Church to keep the doors open. True movements are made of men and women, who have a passion to be like Jesus where they live, work, study, shop and hang out with people who will repeat the same process. Unless you're making disciples who make disciples of others, you're limited in how fully you're becoming like Jesus.

Jesus taught and lived this mission, as did his disciples. Christianity went viral throughout the then known world and continued until Christianity became the state religion. Then things began to become institutionalized, and we ended up with an irrelevant Church, much of it far from Christ and discipling. Any sort of revival took place because God used the gifts he gave to make disciples throughout the Church.

Author and researcher Sam Metcalf has spent his life studying the movements of Christianity. In his book, *Beyond the Local Church: How Apostolic Movements Can Change the World*, Metcalf concludes that most of these movements were started by catalytic individuals who were passionate about their cause and used the principle of making disciples who make disciples. He writes:

> *Both communism and extreme Islamic fundamentalism are evil counterfeits of the movement dynamics deeply embedded in the Christian movement from its very beginning. Jesus himself modeled these dynamics, and the book of Acts is a fascinating textbook on how his followers lived them out in the first century.*[2]

Too often, Metcalf explains, the local church is more concerned about propagating itself rather than reaching the world for Christ through making disciples who make disciples. He astutely argues that to create viral disciple-making movements "...*there are usually three things that come together: 1) the right people, 2) the right structures; and 3) the sovereign anointing of God.*"[3]

Carrying out Jesus' Great Commission to make disciples of all nations (Matt. 28: 18-20) will only happen as we become disciples who make disciples that make disciples. At its core, this movement must be empowered by God's presence through his Spirit—free of the Western Church's prevailing structures that are really just designed to produce programs and professionals who run the programs and do ministry. Instead, it's up to us to look for new ways to create structures and opportunities that equip, empower and release people to be disciples who are freed up to make disciples who make disciples.

Living On Through the Disciples You Reproduce

One last comment on why you should want to be a disciple maker: All of us will die. That's a guarantee! Of course, we don't dwell on this thought, but the reality is that this life we're privileged to live *will t*erminate. We all need an exit strategy. Though few of us think much about what will happen once we're gone, many psychologists agree that one of our greatest needs is a desire to live on, or at least leave a mark of significance. The wisest of us will plan for our legacy.

Scripture reveals that in eternity, what really matters is our souls *and the souls of others.* The soul work we do within ourselves lasts forever (being a disciple), and the soul work we do in others (making disciples) will last for eternity. As many of us seek to make a significant contribution to our world, the energy you invest in others will last forever. Jesus paints a clear picture of this in Matthew 25, as he tells what is commonly referred to as the Parable of the Talents. Immediately after this passage, we find Jesus telling the Parable of the Sheep and Goats.

Matthew's text reveals the importance of investing what we have been given in this life to impact our eternity and the eternities of others. We've all been given time, talents and treasures that we can spend in a variety of ways. Taken together, these two parables point to the importance of investing our resources to become disciples and care for those less fortunate. We are called to invest our resources in others who then maximize our return for eternal purposes.

Our hope is that reading this book will inspire you to make disciples who become disciple makers themselves. In this way, you'll multiply your life and legacy, ultimately impacting generations of disciples for eternity—well beyond your personal reach.

Chapter 2

CAN ANY CHRISTIAN BE A DISCIPLE MAKER?

Jesus clearly stated his expectation that *all* of his followers would grow and make disciples (Matt. 28:19-20). He didn't select a few special individuals and set out to change the world through them. Rather, he chose a wide variety of people of all walks and stations in life. They all became disciples who made disciples in their own way. They were professionals, housewives, prostitutes, tradesmen, and politicians, rich and poor.

Not Personality Dependent

As we look at those who made disciples in the New Testament, it's clear that disciple making isn't limited to certain personality types, careers, callings, or ages. We don't really know the variety of vocations and personality types in the New Testament, but we know that:

- Peter—was outspoken and impulsive.
- Barnabas— was warm and accepting.
- Lydia— was a risk taker and hospitable.
- Paul— was dominant and direct.
- Timothy—was withdrawn and reserved.
- Mary— was busy and meticulous.
- Apollos— was studious and reflective.
- Titus— was organized and strategic.

- Thomas— was skeptical and detailed.
- Luke— was educated and analytical.

So often today, people qualify certain personality traits, saying that those who have those traits are better than others at making disciples. This is a lie from the evil one. The enemy of our soul would like nothing better than to convince you that you can't make disciples because _____ (you fill in the blank). Many of us have rehearsed tapes of why we we're not that good at making disciples. Too often, we put up objections and excuses in an attempt to explain that God can't use us to make disciples of others.

Before we go any further, let's first establish the point that *you* aren't the one making a disciple. in John 14:16, Jesus is pretty clear that disciple making is the role of the Spirit who does the transforming work within someone. Only through the power and presence of the indwelling Spirit does God use us to impact another. We're simply partnering with him in the process. God could surely make disciples without us (he is God), but for our benefit, he has chosen us to walk beside him in the process of transforming a life.

Recently, some friends we (Greg) hadn't heard from or seen in almost thirty years visited my wife, Mary Kay, and me. We were so thankful they intentionally sought us out after all these years. As we sat on our back porch laughing and sharing memories of the past, there came a point when it was obvious they had something important to tell us. They grew serious and told us the reason they looked us up was to tell us what a powerful impact we had made in their lives, discipling them as a young married couple.

Their words blew us away as they recalled event after event that happened over two years in this group we led. Mary Kay and I had been intentional about focusing on being disciples who would make disciples that make disciples. As we listened in awe, we were moved to tears. We all were. We had no clue the Spirit was making such impact in their lives through us. Only after they left, did Mary Kay and I look at each other and confess that we didn't even remember them being in that group! That night, they had shared so many details only someone in the group would have known, so we knew they were in our group. But we had little memory of that experience.

The power and presence of the Spirit is often like that. He takes our obedience and uses it to do his work. He works in unfathomable ways unbeknownst to us. In the quiet corners of homes and hearts, the Spirit does his transformational work. Don't think that God's ability to work through you is limited to your personality or position. Most often, he will work through or around these.

Ironically, we can both tell you that the disciples that have grown through our investments entrusted by the Spirit grew more through intentional relationships than any sermon or service we led as pastors. Earlier, as Greg shared in Chapter 1, we often had to intentionally make disciples *in spite of* being pastors. We both feel it was often harder to make disciples as a pastor than it was as a layperson.

Unique to Your Gifts, Passions and Walk with Christ

Your ability to make disciples is not dependent on personality, position, knowledge, education, age ethnicity, background, season of life, or your score on this disciple maker assessment. Your disciple-making ability is not dependent on your gifts, passions and walk with Christ. There are surely some particularities about you that influence *how* you make disciples, but surely not *if* you make them.

Making a disciple is about communicating Christ's transformational principles in the context of a relationship. Simply put, you can give someone something that you don't have. We believe (and Scripture backs us up) that it's best for someone to experience the power and presence of Christ personally before the Spirit uses him to disciple others. God surely can do it without such. But he simply chooses to work through willing and intentional vessels— yes, often broken ones.

If your gifts are more "behind-the-scenes," then you'll most often find yourself working with others in those kinds of relationships. Both of our wives, Mary Kay and Cindy, do not see themselves as public speakers; they prefer staying out of the spotlight. In fact, they'll be unhappy with us using them to illustrate this point, but they're perfect examples. With both Mary Kay and Cindy, you'll often find them helping others, serving in the kitchen, or cleaning up after special times with people we have in our homes.

However, God has used each woman to impact many people. Some are young people who have either stayed with us for a few months or others who have met with us from time to time. When people stay with us, Mary Kay and Cindy do as Paul did; they share their life and the gospel as well. People see them living out Jesus' words and loving others through their gifts. They share naturally in context of the relationships that God brings them.

Mary Kay's and Cindy's methods stand in direct contrast to our methods. Greg and I are much more upfront and love working with individuals that desire to be used of God to lead. Though our methods differ greatly from our wives', we work well together. We are keenly aware of these differences, so we disciple differently in various arenas. One is no better than the other—just different.

We chose Mary Kay and Cindy as examples because too often people who are not gifted in strong teaching or leadership gifts feel inadequate as disciple makers. In the remaining sections of this book, we talk about the different levels of disciple making. The goal of using these levels is not to label and/or judge. Rather, we want to help you assess and understand where you are as a disciple maker so that God can use you to a greater degree in expanding his Kingdom.

It doesn't matter what your gifts are; you're called to make disciples. The challenge will be different for each of us. We guarantee that regardless of your position, gifts, education or stage in life, you *will* struggle with prioritizing your life to make disciples and not just do church work. But you *can* do it!

For example, pastors of large churches will struggle with setting priorities over the long term to continue pouring into leaders to make disciples. There is a great temptation to only disciple those who can benefit the church whom you serve. We know. We've been there. But often, leaders who become disciples of Jesus who then make disciples will be called of God to do that elsewhere. Think of Barnabas and Paul (Acts 13). If and when that happens, we must release these leaders to such places. This is multiplication. We're not just planting churches or sites, but rather, discipling people who can make disciples of others who can then lead churches in multiplication.

The goal of multiplying churches isn't simply having more institutional churches on the corners of our communities, but rather to have more bodies of Christ that are committed to, and are practicing, disciple making. Are you discipling people who have the time and interest in making disciples of Christ? That is effective multiplication. in his book, *Becoming a Level Five Multiplying Church*, Exponential Director Todd Wilson looks at why and how disciple making is core to Kingdom multiplication.[1] Disciple making must be the backbone of churches that are growing and multiply.

Try reading Acts and the Epistles through the eyes of Paul. He poured into a large number of men and women, yet most left him to be involved in other ministries. Some had conflict with him; some turned on and even hurt him. At the end of his life, in the last chapter of 2 Timothy, Paul asks Timothy to bring Mark and to come to him. We don't know if they ever made it to Paul, but it's no surprise that during his final days on earth, Paul would want to be with those he had invested in and in whom he had multiplied himself. This kind of reminds us of Matthew 28 when Jesus called his disciples to himself.

Making disciples of individuals is not an easy endeavor; nothing that changes this world ever is.

CHAPTER 3

WHY DEVELOP AN ASSESSMENT TOOL?

Disciple makers struggle to find common markers and common vernacular to describe the process of disciple making. This was the goal in developing a commonly available assessment tool focused on disciple making. Establishing a common vernacular and common markers of the varied approaches to discipleship will be beneficial for the community of disciple-making disciples. Our online tool is designed to help Christians develop an objective assessment of themselves as disciple makers. By establishing profiles and criteria, we create a benchmark—an objective standard that helps us compare our standard with that of today's effective disciple makers.

Once you establish a base level, you'll be able to assess ways to grow and improve. Essentially, you'll gain a sense of the necessary resources for helping you on your journey to become the best possible disciple maker. That is the ultimate goal for developing this tool—to help each person in his or her journey make disciples as Jesus made disciples who then made disciples.

The online assessment offers five basic levels that are not as much theological in orientation (Kingdom, church, etc.,) as they are practical and measurable. This is an important point. We're *not* saying our model is taught in Scripture. Rather, it's a model that we find to be in step with what the Bible teaches. The distinction is important.

We have followed the general outline that aligns with Scripture, but our assessment tool is more descriptive of what we find practically in the lives of disciple makers today. We think you'll find it helpful and biblical, but we would not bind it on others as God's standard. Again, this is not to say that our model lacks theological support—far from it. A deeper analysis shows that our model has much in common with the disciple-making practices described in the Bible and by Jesus himself, as the discipleship scholar, Robert Coleman, laid out many years ago.[1]

Five Disciple Maker Profiles

The goal of this assessment tool is to help you determine your personal level of maturity and competency in being used by God to effectively build up others in their relationship with Christ, and to develop their own ability to do this with others. This is what the Apostle Paul encouraged Timothy to do when he wrote: *"And the things you have heard me say in the presence of many witnesses entrust to reliable people who will also be qualified to teach others"* (2 Tim. 2:2). This is commonly called the process of making disciples who make disciples.

This tool measures your level of effectiveness in making disciples. Once you understand where you currently are in this lifelong process, you can intentionally grow in ways to improve your effectiveness on this journey. Our goal is to help each person become a better disciple maker throughout his or her life.

For simplicity, we have developed this tool so that most individuals will fit into one of the five disciple maker profiles. These profiles are practical and measurable ways of classifying where you are in the process. The five stages are not intended to be a label that describes you as an individual, but rather a brief snapshot of five levels of behavior described in this assessment tool. For simplicity's sake, we grouped these behaviors into five categories to help you understand and apply them.

The Five Levels of Disciple Making

Level 1—These disciple makers demonstrate the behaviors of people who are not passionate about growing in their relationship with Christ through obedience to Jesus' disciple-making call. They don't personally or intentionally focus on helping others grow in their relationship with Christ, and they don't help others make disciples. They may actually have a negative impact on disciple making because they allow the world to have a greater impact on the people around them than they do for the cause of Christ.

Level 2—The behaviors of this group describe those who identify with Christ but are not yet growing in their relationship with him. Similar to Level 1, they are not personally making disciples. However, they do help in disciple-making efforts by attempting to be a regular part of group meetings or gatherings that involve others who are growing and becoming disciples. The behaviors of these men and women prevent disciple making from progressing as quickly as the next three levels (3, 4 and 5) because those assessing at Level 2 don't seek to intentionally influence others for spiritual growth.

Level 3—These behaviors describe disciple makers who intentionally advance the disciple-making efforts of others by serving and aiding in the group activities and gatherings of the body of Christ. They are loyal to their local church, his body and to the leaders who promote disciple making. They are personally growing in their relationship with Christ and can be described as spiritually minded individuals who know what they believe. They can be depended on in groups and gatherings for the cause of disciple making and may personally make small steps toward making disciples of others and inviting others into the disciple-making activities of the church.

Level 4—These behaviors describe disciple makers who are intentionally growing and are actively making disciples. They personally invest in relationships so that they can make disciples and assist in others' disciple-making efforts as well. They are committed to the process of disciple making personally, do it themselves, and join with the leaders of their church or para-church organizations to lead people and groups. They live to see disciples made through their efforts.

Level 5—The behaviors of this disciple maker describe someone who is a mature disciple maker—intentional and effective at raising up not just new disciples, but also new disciple makers. Those assessing at Level 5 have a long-term view of God's Kingdom, well beyond the level of their own influence. They live to develop individuals who will make disciple makers who will then make other disciple makers, many of whom they will never meet. They are fully engaged in igniting and fueling disciple-making movements within their church or fellowship of churches.

Each level of these disciple makers is unique; their practices vary greatly. But they all have common ways of thinking about God, people, being a disciple, the Kingdom, and what it means to make disciples of Jesus.

Intentionality Matters

Bill Hull is a leader who has given his life to mastering disciple making. He has written more than twenty books on the topic and has established two international networks that help leaders implement disciple making in their ministries. He is one of the leaders who has helped us develop and test this online assessment, as well as contributed his insights to this book. After reviewing the assessment, he asked us to clarify something for our readers that many, especially younger people, might find to be a helpful insight. He stressed the need for intentionality.

If we want to truly love people like Jesus did, Bill said, we will learn to practice intentionality. Our commitment to intentionality expresses our love for whomever we're praying for and discipling. In fact, it seems to be the biggest difference maker between those who just *aspire* to making disciples and those who actually do it effectively. This online assessment will help you gauge how you're doing at embracing intentionality as *the Spirit's primary way* for making disciple. God's Spirit works through us, helping us to use our minds and develop wise strategy.

We anticipate that there will be people who may initially dislike the fact that we have identified and defined "levels" of disciple making. Or they may dislike the fact that we categorize, organize and prioritize disciple making. We encourage you to resist the urge to reject intentionality. Embrace that principle. This assessment tool will help you examine and evaluate yourself and then help you find and employ the best next-step plans—helping you become more effective at championing the greatest cause on planet Earth.

The Mathematics of Impact

We can view and understand these profiles by looking at their mathematical impact, which means we frame the tool through the lenses of subtraction, addition, and multiplication. For example, at Level 1, a disciple maker actually has a negative impact on the cause of disciple making. Stated differently, the cause of Christ often loses because of their influence. They either give a bad name to the cause of Christ, or their influence is the same as the world's. These are the undeveloped Christians, those who do not act like they know Christ. Their lives often show no fruit. They may be called hypocrites and fakes. They *subtract* from disciple-making effectiveness.

But now let's now go up to say, Level 3. Here, we find disciples who help add disciples and add to disciple-making efforts. They are supportive, hard-working members of a local body or para-church. They help add people to the Kingdom because they provide a place for others to come and receive influence from disciple makers in groups and gatherings (for example, church services). They are the people who get there for the services, make it to the small group or class meetings, serve, help, and can be counted on to support the leadership of group disciple makers. They also are likely to invite their friends and acquaintances to church. Not only will they work hard, they will also provide financial and personal support for disciple-making activities. Their efforts help add disciples and help disciples grow.

Now let's jump to Level 5, which is all about multiplication. These disciple makers have become so effective that those they raise up become disciple makers. Their disciples train and readily transfer what they've learned to other disciples who, in turn, take the same practices that have been passed on to them and replicate what they have gained with others. This is the ideal that Jesus established with His disciples. They became disciples who made disciples who made disciples. Their efforts have a multiplying effect.

In practice, these levels of subtraction, addition, and multiplication will overlap and blend because we're dealing with people. All of us are complex individuals. Those complexities don't go away in our lives as disciples and disciple makers. There can be spurts of growth and influence and then periods of decline and waning influence.

The boundaries may not always be clear. Between a negative impact on disciple making (Level 1) and adding to the disciple-making efforts of others (Level 3), we can plateau as disciple makers (Level 2). Or between adding to disciple-making efforts (Level 3) and being a multiplying influencer (Level 5), someone may just be a faithful disciple maker who reproduces disciples, yet their disciples never become disciple makers themselves (Level 4).

The following image illustrates the overlaps and the five levels of disciple making:

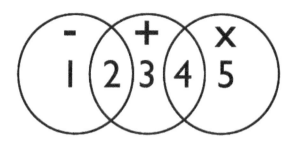

Level: Subtracting // Level 2: Plateauing // Level 3:
Adding // Level 4: Reproducing // Level 5: Multiplying

Let's get practical. For example, let's envision someone who fits into Level 3. Look at the following five bullet points that could characterize Level 3 disciple making (Note that because of the overlaps we just discussed, not all will apply to every person at Level 3):

- The disciple maker's mindset is truly oriented to God's Kingdom (he is a spiritual young adult).
- The disciple maker may have personally made efforts to disciple others but without much effectiveness.
- No one has intentionally trained the disciple maker in how to personally disciple others.
- The disciple maker supports disciple-making efforts by serving and financially providing resources for others who are making disciples.
- The disciple maker will help, support, and do what she can for the Kingdom of God.

The Disciple-Making Profiles (Levels 1-5)

We can describe each of the five levels of disciple making by identifying and defining certain attributes or characteristics that work together to reveal five separate profiles. Our team of national disciple-making leaders met, prayed and labored over describing each level to help distinguish and separate it from the other four. This wasn't always easy. We also fully appreciate that everyone will not agree with every characteristic. However as we went through many revisions, we found that the following bulleted characteristics do provide a place to begin understanding each of the five levels of disciple making.

The characteristics are our attempt to behaviorally, attitudinally or spiritually describe each level so that anyone can clearly understand which profile they would fit in based on the specific lists of characteristics.

Level 1 Profile:

- Claims conversion, but shows no or little fruit of it.
- Shows little biblical or God impact in their lives.
- Is uninformed about the faith.
- Exhibits a lack of obedience.
- Demonstrates a lack of Christlike character.
- Doesn't serve in the church.
- Has a consumer mentality.
- Has no personal ministry.
- Has no accountability, intimate transparency or relationships.
- Seeks little to no communication with God (prayer).
- Shows no life of repentance.
- Loves the world more than Jesus (demonstrated by their actions, though they won't say it).
- Is a poor example of a follower of Christ.
- Is a Christian by self-identification but not a disciple.
- Wrong scorecard messes up their life and the lives of those around them.

Level 2 Profile:

- Is self-centered but wants to grow some and may be involved in a church or small group.
- Thinks about himself first, then others.

- Has a poor discipline for godliness.
- Knows very little of God's heart.
- Is biblically illiterate.
- Views the world from a human perspective.
- Views others from a worldly perspective.
- Has no personal ministry using his gifts.
- May go to church, but is a spectator, not a participant.
- Shows a consumer mentality (they come to church to receive rather than contribute).
- Lacks healthy relationships, which causes conflict and division.
- Focuses on himself but wants to get closer to Jesus.

Level 3 Profile:

- Desires what God wants.
- Is growing in relationship with Christ.
- Is committed to Jesus and His Church.
- Simply does not know how to make a disciple of another person.
- Is motivated to make disciples but lacks confidence and competence.
- Is viewed as a fruitful Christian.
- Has a lack of reproduction in personally making disciples of others.
- May have some quiet disappointment in their inability to make disciples.
- Is involved in programs but lacks intentional disciple-making relationships.
- Supports their church and its institutional needs.
- Discipleship is a defined small group study rather than a lifestyle.
- Needs a church to help others grow.
- Practices various disciplines that encourage her own growth in Christ.
- Seeks to be a good model of a follower of Christ.

Level 4 Profile:

- Focuses on Jesus and what he desires.
- Enjoys helping others spend time with Jesus through studying his Word.
- Believes and practices disciple making.
- Reproduces the life of Jesus in one or more people at a time.
- Practices grace-centered accountability in her relationships.
- Demonstrates a bias to "yes," meaning she encourages her disciples to try new things.
- Loves others as they are, but influences them to be more than they were.
- Understands the reproducing process and practices it.
- Shows others how to obey the teachings of Jesus.
- Has a good working knowledge of Scripture.
- Creates "life space" or "margin" to be a disciple maker:
  - Time
  - Energy
  - Resources
- Trained in disciple-making models that work (evangelism and discipleship).
- Has a strong personal desire and commitment to serve as a disciple maker.
- Thinks about reproducing themselves through others.

Level 5 Profile:

- Focuses on long-term Kingdom impact through multiple generations.
- Builds intentional relationships with others who will build disciples of others.
- Has a fluid working knowledge of Scripture.
- Coaches others.
- Humility, obedience and servanthood are modeled in those they invest in.
- Trains those they disciple to be spiritual parents.

- Lives a transparent life with those they disciple.
- Driven by Kingdom love, which causes great sacrifice.
- Uses the "imitate me" model, like the apostle Paul did.
- Has a reproducible mindset that allows everything they teach to be replicated by others.
- Is explicit about the process they use to make disciples.
- Champions others who make disciples.
- Builds a leadership pipeline of disciples who make disciples.
- Lives strategically to make disciples who make disciples.
- Has the freedom to live accordingly.

CHAPTER 4

WHY SHOULD I ASSESS MY DISCIPLE-MAKING ABILITY?

So why would we create a tool to assess your disciple-making ability? More importantly, why should you spend the time to take (and act on) the assessment? In conducting assessments for more than twenty-five years, there's one thing that I (Greg) have learned about helping people understand their unique attributes through these assessment tools:

You can never figure out where you want to go unless you first know where you are.

In other words, you need clarifying perspective. Each assessment we create is designed to help you understand your reality. Well-designed assessments provide psychometrically valid insights to help individuals fully appreciate who they are now. Once there, it's feasible to determine where to go and how to get there. Without exception, assessments help you see yourself more realistically.

It would be foolish to set out driving with no sense of where you are or where you want to go. Think about your GPS and how it gets you to where you want to go. A GPS must first locate your current position and then locate the desired address or location. Only then can the GPS plot the specific steps that you must take to get to your destination.

In life, you may have different options to get to where you're going. It may surprise you to learn that what helps in putting together a path to your preferred future is knowing where you have been. For this reason, the Disciple Maker Assessment evaluates your *past, present* and *future aspirations* as three separate perspectives.

Recently, I (Greg) was coaching a pastor who was struggling with his fear of failing to be a successful disciple maker. As it turned out, this pastor's fear was rooted in family history so I reminded him of the importance of understanding our past before plotting our future. In other words, in your pursuit of becoming a disciple maker it's helpful to understand where you've been. Of course, this assessment is not about understanding "how" you developed your past disciple-making behavior; that's beyond the scope of this book and/or tool. We are only evaluating actual behaviors from your past.

Measuring disciple-making levels is not an attempt to guilt anyone, but rather an opportunity to take an honest look at yourself. As with any assessment, "fudging" or painting a rosy picture of a past that really didn't exist does no one any good. When you're honest about where you've been, you can then better evaluate where you currently are. Let me suggest that if you want to be someone who will consistently improve as a disciple maker, you need to know not only where you are, but also where you have been in regard to individual goals.

> *Understanding where you've been (past) enables you to figure out where you are (present).*

A few years ago, I (Bobby) spent time with a key leader in our church who had a deep passion to become a better disciple maker. We actually fasted and prayed together, asking God to bring just the right person into Kevin's life so that he could lead them to Christ and help them to grow in Christ (remember, disciple making is both evangelism and sanctification). Kevin was a Level 3 disciple maker—supporting, tithing, and serving in our church. His desire was strong, but desire wasn't enough. He needed to understand the specifics of what you do as a spiritual parent (Level 4). Objective assessments like this tool not only help people understand where they're currently at, they're also training tools to help people discover pathways forward. This assessment can open your eyes to attitudes, perspectives and strategies that you can develop.

As I (Greg) worked on developing this tool, I realized that I have gone through seasons of life where I made disciples; other seasons where I made disciples who made disciples; and finally some seasons where I actually have made disciples who made disciples who then made disciples. These realizations were important in helping me understand my past practice of making disciples because now I can better understand where I currently am in making disciples and why.

This "past" perspective also helps me plot out a path of what I need to do to be where I want to be. Whether you're new to the Christian faith or have years of experience to lean on, reflect on your predominant behaviors for the last two to five years as you take the assessment.

Understanding where you are (present) enables you to figure out how to get to where you want to be (future).

To determine your current perspective, as with your past, the assessment evaluates your behavior in disciple making over the course of the last twelve months. Most of us tend not to separate our beliefs from our behavior, but these are two very different constructs for all of us. As you respond to the items within any assessment, make sure you answer based upon your behaviors—what you've actually *done* rather than what you *believe.*

Most of us believe in the Church. Specifically, those of us who are devoted Christ followers should be known as disciple makers. However, very few actually practice this as a way of life through our behaviors. The only way we can address behaviors in a positive and proactive manner is to acknowledge where we are, both in the past and currently. There is a huge difference in belief and behaviors—what we aspire to do versus what we actually practice. Ironically, when you Google the difference between practices and beliefs, you get more than 29 million hits with the large majority of them associated with religious beliefs. You must get honest about where you are, and the gap between your present and where you want to go.

> *Understanding where you want to be enables you to move in that direction (future).*

In this assessment, we'll ask you about your future or aspirational behavior as a disciple maker. What behaviors would typify your life as a disciple who makes disciples that makes disciples? Assessments ask about typical behaviors as an opportunity to take an introspective look at yourself, so it's important to respond based on what your heart desires. Avoid answering based on what others want for you; think hard about what you really desire. Trying to please others won't really be enough motivation to cause you to change, much less reorient, your life. Answering in a manner that isn't rooted in reality is just not helpful.

In regard to your future perspective and the level you aspire to be: most of us reading this book probably have some concept of our calling to make disciples. We may not have understood our need to make disciple makers until now, but most of us knew we should at least be making disciples. We may lack the internal discipline and the know-how. That's okay. Life is messy. We don't always respond the way we desire. It's truly God at work in and through us who produces a disciple who makes disciples. Our role is to aspire to Level 5 and then cooperate with the Holy Spirit to get there.

Aspiring to Level 5

In the early beta testing of the online tool, we discovered a surprising insight. Less than 25 percent of the respondents aspired to be

Level 5 disciple makers! Included in that number are many people in ministerial and pastoral positions. We were surprised, but then after conversations between all of us (Greg, Bobby, and Todd Wilson), the number began to make sense.

The truth is that it is a big step for everyday Christians—and even those in ministry—to aspire to turn desire into actions and become personal disciple makers who make and multiply disciples. Once a leader or a church leadership team starts to emphasize the importance of personal disciple making, getting people to embrace it as a focus (something they practice) requires a lot of teaching, love, and coaching. Most of our respondents felt good about aspiring to just become disciple makers. To them, that represented a big change in their perspective and focus.

But we want to encourage everyone reading this book to go one step further and pursue Level 5 disciple making. Exponential likes to call them Level 5 multipliers or "hero makers." When we make disciple makers (Level 5), we become "hero makers." Those who make disciple makers change the lives of the people they're discipling for eternity. They are making people who will be heroes in eternity.

It is aspiring to be like Jesus. Jesus spent the most important time in his ministry not just making disciples, but making disciple makers out of James, Peter, John, and the rest of the twelve. Those who make disciple makers are imitating Jesus. There is no higher calling.

Evaluating the Results

Once you've invested time to take any assessment, you need to spend time reviewing the results. Most assessments will give you a summary page that's designed to help you investigate options for improvement.

Assessments are not all created equal. This disciple-making assessment has been vetted and is psychometrically valid (applying stats and mathematical techniques to psychological testing). Our hope, our desire, is to help you grow to become more effective by understanding where you were, where you are, and where you want to go in becoming a disciple maker. This assessment is a good start to this lofty and Kingdom-expanding endeavor.

CHAPTER 5

WHAT IS THE SPIRITUAL FAMILY METAPHOR?

As leaders dedicated to the cause of making disciples, we look for multiple ways we can help you understand our assessment tool. For this comparison, we went back to Scripture. As we mentioned earlier, we want to be careful not to bind our model on people, as though it's biblical doctrine. Yet at the same time, we can draw language from the Bible that matches a physical reality in the world—a metaphor that people can easily associate with and understand. The Bible describes people at different levels of spiritual development using the analogy of family: from infants to children to parents.

The Discipleship Process

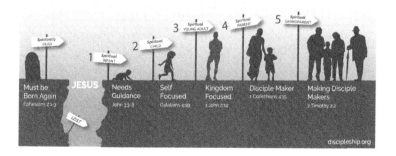

In his book, *The Disciple Maker's Handbook*, Bobby (and his co-writer Josh Patrick) include a chapter that maps out the disciple maker's growth journey.[1] We encourage you to read that book.

The above illustration – shared with us by Discipleship.org identi-fies the five levels of Christians and the spiritual family references that match each level. This developmental concept is new to many, especially to those who have been taught that salvation is a one-time event or to those who have not been taught the biblical un-derstanding of development and growth. It is a vitally important framework in disciple making and the core reproducible process used by Jim Putman and other leaders in the Relational Disciple-ship Network.[2]

As we introduce this family concept, we want to make two things clear. The previous illustration presents a clear, linear pro-gression of growth. But as we talked about in chapter 4, it doesn't always work this way in real life. The discipleship journey may not be linear; at times, it's up and down, back and forth. It often looks either very messy or stagnant. *And no two journeys are the same.* This illustration is useful in that it clearly outlines the growth pro-cess. We can see general principles at work, but the contours of each person's journey with Jesus are sacred and one of a kind.

Second, someone can be an infant and still have a very signifi-cant impact as a disciple maker shortly after becoming a Christian. If someone is disciplined and responsible with habits of commit-ment and follow up, an infant can appear to be a spiritual young adult, or even a parent. In a strictly mathematical model, infants can positively influence disciple making right away. But the key thing that matters, over the long haul, is inner transformation. Just like physical children can act beyond their maturity level for a limited period of time, those who are spiritually young can do the same. We can expect this. However if we expect this to be the norm, there will be problems.

Someone who has developed a love for God and his Kingdom over time will serve not just out of responsibility and good char-acter—they will serve from a transformed heart and mind. Their service won't be based just on skills—but also the development of a mindset and heart for God. Because such growth has come from the Holy Spirit, truly mature people are less likely to impose immature or unwise standards on those they're discipling.

Keep the family model in mind as you read the rest of this chapter. We'll start with spiritual infants and then move on to describe the development of disciple makers up through being parents and grandparents. A grandparent, as we'll see, has multiple generations of disciples and disciple makers. We can often find an organic correlation between the disciple maker levels and the spiritual family:

- Spiritual infants = Level 1 disciple makers
- Spiritual children = Level 2 disciple makers
- Spiritual young adults = Level 3 disciple makers
- Spiritual parents = Level 4 disciple makers
- Spiritual grandparents = Level 5 disciple makers

The single biggest predictor of development from levels 3 to 4 and from levels 4 to 5 is intentionality. Let us be like Bill Hull and stress that word again: *disciple makers are guided by intentionality.* When we're intentional, we're deliberate or purposive. Intentionality requires us to have and follow a plan; it's knowing where to take people and how to help them get there. Yes, God's Spirit is at work in and through the process, however intentionality opens the door for this transformative process to take place.

Stage One—Infant (Lacking Knowledge)

Spiritual infants are newborn Christians (Heb. 5:12–14). Just like babies need to be cared for and given milk, spiritual infants need lots of care. They're not yet ready for solid food. They don't have in-depth spiritual knowledge, developed habits, and maturity. They don't have the capacity to make disciples of others from a spiritual foundation. They can learn skills and processes, but they will not last without internal growth.

When people are spiritual infants, their words and actions reveal the truth of who they are. You often hear one or more of the following from infants:

- God wants us to be tolerant and accepting of everything and everyone.
- Jesus, Allah, Buddha, and Karma are all talking about the same principles.
- I had no idea the Bible said that!
- I want to be a good Christian, but I don't want to leave my former life behind.
- I don't really have time for church, and I'm too busy to be involved.

I (Bobby) just received my first grandchild into the world. Wow, what a great joy! But I had forgotten how much care and attention an infant requires. I spent a whole day watching him recently, and it just about wore me out.

In the same way, it's a great joy to see a newborn spiritual infant. But we easily miss that they, too, need a lot of care and attention. They need protection, nurturing and guidance. They need someone to show them what the Bible teaches and how they should now live. They need role models that they can respect and follow.

If spiritual infants are nurtured and guided in the context of relationship, then they can grow. That's why we need to commit to the hard work of parenting. Infants especially need disciple makers whom they can respect and can model their lives after.

Stage Two—Child (Self-Focused but Growing)

In 1 Thessalonians 2:10–12, Paul describes himself as a spiritual father dealing with his children—encouraging, comforting, and urging them to live lives worthy of God. People in the "child" stage are growing in their relationship with God and beginning to grow in their relationships with other Christians. But like all children, they are naturally self-centered. And they continue to need considerable nurturing and guidance.

For disciple makers, this stage is important to understand. God designed human beings so that they grow up through the childhood stage. As a child develops, it's necessary for his or her development to go through this period with a high focus on personal needs. It helps children differentiate themselves from their parents and sets them up for young adulthood, where they can naturally become more focused upon others.

Disciple makers can be easily frustrated by the self-focus of spiritual children. For example, children often only want to be in a small group if they can get something out of it. They can focus on their desire for good preaching, programs, and praise and can come off as consumers of religious goods and services.

This posture should not surprise us. Children are like that. We need to be careful that we avoid becoming judgmental when spiritual children act like children. It's natural for a Christian to process through a childhood phase on the way to becoming a spiritual young adult or parent. Of course, we challenge this behavior, but we do it with love and grace. Some will respond to our guidance and direction. Others will not.

Remember, when we understand that growth as a disciple is a journey and a process, we can have appropriate expectations of those we're discipling. At this stage, you might hear someone say:

- The pastor's sermons aren't feeding me.
- I would love to attend church regularly, but I don't have time.
- I don't really want to go to small group because I would like friends who are more like myself.
- I can't believe that a good God would allow such pain to come into my life.

People in this growth stage need to learn to do the right things for the right reasons, no matter how they feel. This is where a person will begin to experience some growing pains and may at first be tempted to avoid pain or conflict. They may be emotionally immature as well. Discipling someone involves modeling maturity and teaching him to cultivate a servant's versus self-centered heart.

Once a true Kingdom focus and a servant's heart begin to develop, he moves into the young adult phase.

Stage Three—Young Adult (Kingdom-Focused)

In 1 John 2:13–14, we find a description of spiritual young men. John tells us that they have overcome the evil one, and the Word of God abides in them. This is a big step in Kingdom effectiveness. Spiritual young adults are recognizable because they're shifting from self-centeredness to being God-centered and others-centered. In this stage of spiritual development, it's a joy to disciple people. The Spirit is transforming their hearts, and the Kingdom of God is real to them.

When I (Bobby) served as a lead pastor in Calgary, Canada (my home city), I had the privilege of leading a middle-aged man named Greg (not Greg, my co-author) to faith in Christ. I was amazed at his earnestness for the faith. We often studied the Bible together, met for lunch, shared our lives, and became good friends. Over time, I saw Greg grow.

I will never forget the day that it hit me how much he had grown spiritually. He and his wife had arrived at our Sunday gathering early. He was there to serve. His whole life was revolving more and more around service.

One day I was down the hall from where Greg was, and I overheard him talking to his wife. He gave her a report on all the things that were going on in the church and then he said, "Isn't it great how things are going and everything that's happening in the church?" Greg was now a young adult. And I was grateful to watch his journey.

Here are some things you often hear people say at the young adult stage:

- I am so grateful for all that God has done for me.
- I really want to make a difference and for my life to count for God's Kingdom.

- I find it such a joy to financially support my church and give back to God.
- Ben and Tiffany weren't at our group last week; I'm going to find out if they're okay.
- I wish I could hear more sermons to grow.
- I plan to be at church, and I will help with whatever they need.

Young adults are a joy for church leaders. But please note, it's easy for church leaders to rely on such people for their support of the church and her programs. We rely on these people and unconsciously keep them in their place of service. They can often get so busy doing things at church that they do not have or make time to develop to the next level and become personal disciple makers. If they don't grow to the next level after years of serving, they will often become stunted and unfulfilled.

Stage Four—Parent (Intentional Disciple Maker)

Physical parents will often state it as a fact: there is just nothing like parenting to help you grow up. And nothing gives people more joy than their children and seeing them do well. In Galatians 4:10, Paul describes what it's like to be a spiritual parent. He calls the Galatians his "dear children," describing his longing and pains, "until Christ is formed" in them. No one parents accidentally. Parenting requires forethought and guidance—and, most importantly, *intentionality* (there's that word again).

A parent understands their children's needs, and they find ways to meet them. They do this personally and relationally. I (Bobby) helped a young man named Kevin learn about disciple making and then guided him through the process of leading his friend, Glen, to place his faith in Jesus. It was a great day!

Just as encouraging is the way that Kevin invested in and guided Glen in the months and years after Glen placed his faith in Jesus. For several years, they met every Friday morning to study the Bible, share their lives, and pursue Jesus together. Kevin met

Glen at the point of his need and then guided him, step by step, in the journey of becoming more and more like Jesus. Without a spiritual parent like Kevin, I don't think Glen would be where he is today.

The following statements characterize the parent stage:

- I think Susan may be ready for me to help her make the decision to follow Jesus. I want to ask her to study the Bible with me at lunch.
- I'm burdened for my neighbor. I want to invite him to start meeting with me and join the new men's group I'm forming.
- I'm so happy to lead my group and make disciples. We're going to baptize a new member of our small group tonight!
- The most important discipleship is with my kids. I need encouragement and accountability so that I make it a priority to help them memorize Scripture this week, as we planned.
- I may be the most important person to influence my granddaughter for Jesus. I love meeting with her every two weeks for Bible study.

To become a parent, we often need someone to disciple us in disciple making. But that's not always the case. Many people become spiritual parents by committing to being one, finding the tools for it, and then just doing it, learning as they go. They already have a heart for God. But they need practical models, easy-to-use tools, and reproducible systems. They will also do best with encouragement and ongoing training to help sharpen and hone their skills. The hallmark of a spiritual parent is their intentional mentoring, coaching, and teaching of others. They leverage their influence to help others—ultimately making an eternal difference.

Stage Five—Grandparent (Multiplying Disciple Makers)

Jesus' original intent is that his disciples would make disciples who would make disciples—with a multiplying movement that reaches into every people group on the earth (Matt. 28:19-20). This is Level 5 disciple making. The Book of Revelation pictures Jesus' mission as a fully accomplished reality at the end of history:

After this I looked, and there before me was a great multitude that no one could count, from every nation, tribe, people and language, standing before the throne and before the Lamb. They were wearing white robes and were holding palm branches in their hands (Rev. 7:9).

John's vision is one of legacy. It motivates us to become not just spiritual parents, but also spiritual *grandparents.* With God's help and empowerment, Level 5 disciple makers have multiplied their disciple-making efforts well beyond themselves to people they didn't directly disciple themselves.

In 2 Timothy, Paul encourages Timothy to follow his example and become a spiritual grandparent:

And the things you have heard me say in the presence of many witnesses entrust to reliable people who will also be qualified to teach others (2 Tim. 2:2).

Again, Paul is directing Timothy to not just disciple reliable people. Timothy is to entrust the teaching he received (from Paul) to reliable people, *so they can teach others.* Paul actually pictures disciple making to the fourth generation in this text: Paul is a great-grandparent, who helps Timothy become a grandparent, who helps parents (reliable people) to disciple others!

In many ways, this is an ideal picture for those who are in part-time or full-time ministry as part of a disciple-making church. We personally make disciples, but even more than that, we devote much of our time to making disciple makers who make disciples. At this level, the influence and impact of our ministry extends beyond our direct influence. We move from adding people that we disciple (spiritual parent) to multiplying disciple makers (spiritual grandparent).

The following statements characterize the grandparent stage:

- I'm praying that God will show me who I should invest in and raise up to be disciple makers in this next season.
- I'm so happy to hear that Michelle is going to baptize another person from the group that she's leading. That was our dream when I first started meeting with her a few years ago!
- I'm overwhelmed with thankfulness when I find out about people I don't personally know who have been raised up to become disciple makers by disciple makers I do know.
- My biggest joy is when I hear about multiple generations of disciple makers who were influenced by those I was blessed to disciple and influence.
- I look forward to hearing from Jason. I'm excited to hear about the people God is using him to reach in the disciple-making works he has started since we sent him out.

As we said at the beginning of this chapter, there is often an organic correlation between the stages along the spiritual journey, from infant to grandparent, and the disciple-maker levels, from Level 1 (subtraction) to Level 5 (multiplication). But people are not totally predictable. Some can develop disciple-maker habits at an early spiritual stage, and some can be devout followers of Jesus who never mature past the childhood stage. A person can progress at one level through the steps in a few years, but then regress backward.

But we have found, over time, as a general path, there is a correlation between the spiritual family development phases and the five levels. This is good news! It means that spiritual growth, over time, should lead people to become more and more like Jesus. And Jesus, more than anyone, was a committed disciple maker.

CHAPTER 6

HOW DO WE APPLY THE RESULTS TO OUR LIVES?

One of the most important keys to the Disciple Maker Assessment tool is that it is for *self-assessment*. When we're honest with ourselves, nobody knows us better than *we know ourselves*. Ideally, we will want to assess our own development in a biblical way. In this way, it's not a judgmental or critical experience, but rather an honest assessment to help us grow. Then we can get information, training and coaching that nurtures us in our development to the next stage as disciple makers.

The results of an assessment should not be seen as good or bad results. It's just a gauge on the natural path of growth. For example, a child should not feel bad because they're a child. Childhood is the stage that comes after infancy; it is a bridge to becoming a young adult. If fact, we often tell children not to grow up too fast. In a similar manner, we want to assure newborn spiritual infants and children that they're in a natural stage of growth—unless they have become stuck in that stage for many years (which should be addressed). If they're healthy, and if they grow, as they should, they will move to the next stage.

To help with your growth, we recommend the following steps. Pursue them prayerfully and in partnership with others. In the ideal, an experienced disciple maker will guide you through this process.

1. Take the online inventory to assess and understand the level you're at as a disciple maker.
2. Become familiar with the five levels of disciple making and the correlated spiritual family development path described in this book (and in *The Disciple Maker's Handbook*[1] and in the book *Real Life Discipleship Training Manual*).[2]
3. Listen to the input from mature disciple makers to help you accurately assess yourself. Seek reliable voices as much as possible to get an objective view.

Once you've determined where you're at in your development as a disciple maker, you can then prayerfully get more resources and coaching and develop a plan for your growth. Make no mistake: you'll need help. Proverbs 15:22 says, *"plans fail for lack of counsel, but with many advisers they succeed."* Get help from those who can walk with you and speak into your life.

The good news is that there is a growing number of resources and organizations that can help you in this pursuit. These resources and networks are too many to list, but we can recommend the following leaders and websites to you (see Appendix B). They have participated in the ministry of discipleship.org and helped us create the online assessment tool. They will also have helpful resources. There are also many other voices and resources available through Internet searches.

ENDNOTES

Introduction

1. Jim Putman and Bobby Harrington, with Robert Coleman, *DiscipleShift: Five Shifts that Help Your Church Make Disciples Who Make Disciples* (Zondervan, 2013). See also, Bobby Harrington, *Relational Discipleship is the Core Mission of the Church* (Discipleship.org, 2013).
2. As described by Robert Coleman in his book, *The Master Plan of Evangelism* (Fleming H. Revell, 1962). This book is the gold standard for analysis of Jesus' disciple-making style.
3. Todd Wilson, *Becoming a Level 5 Multiplying Church* (Exponential Resources, 2016).

Chapter 1

1. See Bill Hull and Bobby Harrington, *Evangelism or Discipleship: Can They Effectively Work Together* (Discpleship.org, 2014).
2. Metcalf, Sam. *Beyond the Local Church: How Apostolic Movements Can Change the World*, InterVarsity Press. Kindle Edition. (p.168).
3. Ibid., p. 170

Chapter 2

1. Todd Wilson, *Becoming a Level 5 Multiplying Church* (Exponential Resources, 2016).

Chapter 3

1. Coleman, Robert. *The Master Plan of Discipleship*, (Fleming H. Revell, 1962).

Chapter 5

1. Bobby Harrington and Josh Patrick, *The Disciple Makers Handbook* (Zondervan, 2017).
2. See Avery Willis, Jim Putman, Brandon Guindon, and Bill Krause, *Real-Life Discipleship Training Manual: Equipping Disciples Who Make Disciples* (Colorado Springs: NavPress, 2010).

Chapter 6

1. Bobby Harrington and Josh Patrick, *The Disciple Makers Handbook* (Zondervan, 2017).
2. Avery Willis, Jim Putman, Brandon Guindon, and Bill Krause, *Real Life Discipleship Training Manual: Equipping Disciples Who Make Disciples* (Zondervan, 2017). This manual is the most helpful tool we have found for training disciple makers. There is no substitute for working through this manual to help you know how to disciple people in practical terms. At Harpeth Christian, we require all of our small group leaders to work through this manual and be thoroughly trained in the process and journey of discipleship.

ABOUT THE AUTHORS

BOBBY HARRINGTON is one of the founders of Renew Network and he is also the founding and lead pastor/minister of Harpeth Christian Church (by the Harpeth River, just outside of Nashville, in Franklin, Tennessee). He is also the co-founder and executive director of Discipleship.org, a national forum and ministry that advocates for Jesus' style of disciple making. Before that, Bobby co-founded the Relational Discipleship Network and served as director of missional leadership with Stadia, a national church planting network. He is a Bible teacher, an experienced church planter, coach of church leaders and the author of several books on discipleship, including the popular title, *DiscipleShift* (with Jim Putman) and the recently released book, *The Disciple Makers Handbook* (with Josh Patrick). Bobby has studied at such places as the University of Calgary and Regent College (in Canada), Asbury Seminary, Harding School of Theology, and Princeton Theological Seminary. He has won camel races in Jordan, cliff-dove in competitions near Fish Creek, Alberta, played chess tournaments in Russia, and he has talked to those who have talked to Elvis (all this may not be true). He has a Doctor of Ministry degree from the Southern Baptist Theological Seminary. He and his lovely wife Cindy (that IS *true*) treasure spending time with their friends, grown children, their spouses, and their grandchild.

GREG WIENS has been assessing leaders and organizations for over 35 years. He has worked with a gamut of organizations ranging in size and interest from Fortune 100 companies and public schools, to small non-profits and churches. His forte is leadership, and his passion is to see the Kingdom expanded through helping leaders understand their unique wiring and their A-Game. He has pastored and planted churches as well as founded a number of organizations. He currently leads two missionally focused organizations: Healthy Growing Churches and Healthy Growing Leaders committed to engaging churches and leaders to multiply. Additionally, Greg has developed more than twenty different assessments for organizations, such as Exponential, World Vision (U.S. and International), ECO and the CHOG. He has also consulted and trained these organizations. He is the founder and chief catalyst for Healthy Growing Churches, an organization that works to multiply healthy churches and leaders through assessments, consultations and partnerships. Greg's vision and catalytic leadership provide the unique formula that HGC uses to transform churches and their leadership. Greg's knowledge and expansive experience in both assessments and leadership, coupled with his pastoral background and understanding of church structure, truly allow HGC to provide a personal and detailed recommendation. Churches in sixteen countries and thirty-five states have benefited from Greg's counsel on leadership refinement, church planting, church health and leadership assessment and development. Greg has co-authored two books: *Dying to Restart* and *Daring to Disciple,* both published in 2017.

Made in the USA
Coppell, TX
31 March 2021

52714193R00039